MW00681170

Anaconda Antics

Written by Barbara Winter
Illustrations by Esme Nichola Shilletto

DOMINIE PRESS
Pearson Learning Group

Editor: Bob Rowland
Author: Barbara Winter
Illustrator: Esme Nichola Shilletto

ISBN 0-7685-0746-4
Printed in Singapore
6 7 8 9 VOZF 12 11 10 09

Dominie
Press
Pearson Learning Group

1-800-321-3106
www.pearsonlearning.com

Table of Contents

Chapter One

Looking for Trouble under the Letter *A*

I clicked through the TV channels, but there was nothing good to watch. I had finished reading my book, and Mom was busy in her office in the basement. Sometimes she goes downtown for a meeting, but most of the time she works on her computer at home. I was bored, but I knew I couldn't bother her while she was working.

When I first had chicken pox, I felt sick and was happy to stay in bed. Now I was almost well and couldn't wait to go back to school. However, Mom had said, "Sorry Max, you're going to have to wait until your spots disappear before you leave the house."

The scabs were very itchy, and it was hard not to scratch them. I needed something to do to take my mind off the itch.

I went into my brother Jake's room to see if he had anything I could play with. I poked around his stuff but found nothing. Then I saw Jake's amazing dictionary sitting on the shelf. It didn't look like a special book, but it was. Uncle Cyrus, from Alaska, had sent it to Jake for his tenth birthday. A penguin had appeared in Jake's closet after he'd touched a picture of a penguin in the dictionary and tapped on it! Amazing, but true. And shortly after that, Mom accidentally summoned a monkey without even knowing it.

Jake had told me never to touch his amazing dictionary, but I figured it would be okay to take a peek. After all, I was sick, and you can't yell at a sick little brother. I lifted the big, heavy book with both hands, sat down at Jake's desk, and opened it.

We had all enjoyed having Penny the penguin and Angel the monkey, but I wondered what it would be like to have a really mean animal. I turned to the beginning and looked at the pictures under the letter *A*. There was an aardvark, a strange-looking animal with a long nose. On another page was an albatross with very wide wings. It looked like it would be fun to handle, but I didn't think it could fly in my room.

Over on the next page I found something really cool—

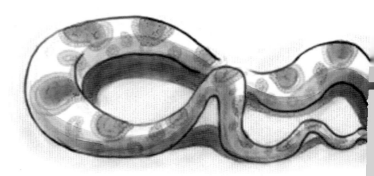

the anaconda. I started to read: "A South American boa, the anaconda is the largest snake in the world. It crushes its prey to death." The picture showed a menacing snake with a long, forked tongue.

Just then, I heard Mom's footsteps on the stairs. I didn't want her to see me with Jake's dictionary, so I quickly jumped up to put it away. I slipped, and my finger dropped onto the page. I froze. Had I touched the picture of the anaconda? I slammed the dictionary shut and shoved it back onto the shelf. Just then, I thought I heard a hissing sound behind me!

Chapter Two

Anaconda on the Loose?

I jumped onto Jake's bed just as Mom came into the room.

"Why are you standing on Jake's bed?" she asked sternly.

"I was looking at his poster of Michael Jordan up close," I told her.

"Get down, Max," Mom snapped. "That's bad for the bed."

I got down on my stomach and bent over to look underneath the bed.

"Now what?" Mom asked.

"I dropped something," I mumbled.

To my relief, there was nothing under the bed. But I was still worried. A snake might have slid somewhere else. I frowned. Mom must have noticed that I was jumpy. She

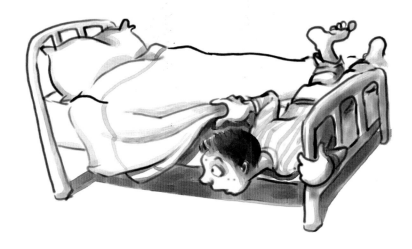

patted my head lightly and said, "Why don't you come downstairs? I've finished my work. I'll make a cup of tea and we can play a card game."

"Okay, I'll be down in a second," I said. "I'll just straighten up Jake's bed."

As soon as Mom left the room, I shut Jake's door. My head was reeling with crazy questions. *If I had called up an anaconda, was it a big one or a baby? Would it fit under doors?* I was really scared. I checked everywhere to make sure there wasn't a snake lurking anywhere. I saw nothing and didn't hear any hissing sounds. Feeling a little better, I went downstairs to look for Mom.

Mom and I played Crazy Eights at the kitchen table. I had trouble concentrating because one thought kept swirling around in my head: *I should have listened to Jake and left the dictionary alone!*

Suddenly an idea came to me. I could send the anaconda back to wherever it had come from! We had sent Penny the penguin and Angel the monkey back by tapping twice on their pictures in the amazing dictionary. I just had to do the same thing again: tap, tap, and the anaconda would disappear.

When the game ended, I yawned and said, "Mom, do you mind if we stop now? I'm feeling sleepy."

"Why don't you take a nap before Jake and Amanda come home?" Mom suggested.

I went straight up to Jake's room. It seemed almost too quiet. First I checked to make sure there wasn't a snake stretched out on the floor or curled up in the closet. Then I grabbed the amazing dictionary and turned to the picture of the anaconda. I tapped it twice.

I wasn't sure if the snake had to be in the same room in order for the magic to work. Penny had been in Jake's closet when she appeared and when she left. Keeping my fingers crossed for luck, I put the dictionary back on the shelf. I hoped the spell had been reversed.

Back in my room, I looked under the bed and inside the closet. I even checked behind the drawers, the bookcase, and under the desk. I didn't see a snake. I lay down on my bed, but I didn't feel very sleepy. I knew I had to tell Jake what had happened when he came home, just in case an anaconda was loose in the house. I closed my eyes, wondering how I was going to tell him, and I dozed off.

Chapter Three

George the Cat Disappears

When I woke up, a giant anaconda was staring at me! Then I heard Jake's loud laugh. He was sitting on my bed, holding up a picture of a large snake in a book.

"Scary, isn't it?" he grinned. "I got this from the library for you—it's a book about snakes."

I grabbed the book and looked at the picture. It was an anaconda!

"Jake, that's an anaconda!" I yelped. "Does it say if anacondas can eat something big? Like eight-year-old guys?"

Jake looked at me as though I were crazy and then read the description under the picture.

"The anaconda can be as long as thirty-six feet. It is olive green with black spots and rings. It lives in trees and water in the hot, damp rainforests of South America."

"But what does it *eat*?" I practically shouted.

Jake read on. "The anaconda eats birds, small mammals, and fish, which it squeezes to death before swallowing."

"I wonder how small they mean?"

"Why this sudden interest in anaconda diets?" Jake asked, suddenly suspicious.

I knew he'd be really mad, but I had to tell him. "I looked in the dictionary today," I confessed.

"You pea brain!" Jake yelled. "You tapped on an anaconda?"

I nodded guiltily. "It was an accident! I don't know if it appeared or not. But I thought I heard something slithering behind me."

"Boy, we're in big trouble if it got out," Jake said. "Have you seen it anywhere?"

"No, but I tried to return it," I said. "I tapped twice on the picture as soon as I could."

"You'd better hope it's gone back," Jake said. "Let's

check to see if it's around anywhere. Maybe it left some tracks when it crawled around."

We inspected Jake's room once more but found nothing. There was no snake, and there were no tracks. We decided it would be safe to go downstairs to watch TV.

When Dad came home from work, he felt my forehead. "Still itching?" he asked.

"Badly," I replied, scratching.

"I think he'll probably be ready to go back to school on Monday," Mom said. "Dinner's ready, everyone. Let's eat."

As we sat down, Dad asked, "Did anyone see the Hamiltons' cat today?"

We shook our heads.

"Why?" Mom asked. "Is he lost?"

"They haven't seen him since last night," Dad said. "The kids were out searching when I came home."

"Poor George," Amanda said.

"Would you call a cat a small mammal, Dad?" I asked.

"Sure." Jake answered for him.

I shuddered.

Jake and Amanda offered to help look for George after dinner.

"Okay, but get home in time to finish your homework," Mom said.

"We will," Jake told her. Then he turned toward me. "Max, you should check *inside* while we're gone."

"I don't think you'll find George in our house," Mom said. "How would he get in?"

"Maybe he slid through when the door was open," Jake said, giving me an angry look.

I got the message.

Chapter Four

Searching for George

After dinner, Amanda and Jake left to join the search for George.

"I'll make sure George isn't in our house," I told Mom and Dad as they settled down in the den with their coffee.

I checked through all the closets in the house, calling loudly, "Here, George, here George." But I was really searching for an anaconda. Finding neither cat nor snake, I flopped down on the sofa and picked up the book that Jake had borrowed for me. Looking at the scary pictures of the anaconda, I was glad we didn't have a cat, especially if an anaconda was sliding around looking for a meal.

Before too long, Jake and Amanda returned, looking frustrated.

"No sign of George," Amanda said. "The Hamiltons are really upset. They're planning a big search of the neighborhood in the morning if George still hasn't returned."

"That's really too bad," Mom said. "What could have happened to the poor cat?"

"Ask Max," Jake muttered.

"You'd better get started on your homework," Mom said to Jake and Amanda. Then she turned to me and ordered, "You—hop in the shower and off to bed."

I was a little nervous as I headed for the bathroom. Before I undressed, I made sure there wasn't a snake slithering in the shower stall or the bathtub.

Back in my room, I conducted another complete inspection. I looked everyplace a snake could possibly hide. I even looked up at the ceiling in case a giant anaconda was coiled around the light. All was clear. I jumped into bed.

Dad and Mom came by to say goodnight. After they'd

shut the door, I stuffed some socks in the gap under my door to keep the anaconda out. Then I climbed into bed, feeling safe and ready to go to sleep. I was exhausted from the tension-filled day.

Just as my eyelids started closing, another thought hit me, and I sat up. If the snake hadn't been sent back, it could be hiding in the heating vents. I looked at the grill on my bedroom floor, and saw with relief that the holes were too small for a snake to get through.

I sank my head into my pillow and pulled my blanket over my eyes, ready to sleep. Then I remembered something else! Jake and I had removed the vent cover in the den to reach for an action figure the day before. Did we put the cover back? I jumped out of bed and ran downstairs to look. The cover was still off! I replaced it, hoping I had trapped the anaconda inside.

When I returned to my room, I lined the socks under
the door again and climbed back into bed. I hoped the
anaconda had returned to the dictionary. I didn't want to
go on living in fear much longer.

Chapter Five

Another Cat Vanishes!

Saturday mornings are quiet at our house, now that hockey season is over. My team finished in first place, but Jake's team didn't do very well. Until soccer starts, Mom and Dad don't have to take us to games and practices.

Dad made us a huge breakfast of eggs, sausages, and pancakes. I couldn't eat much because I was still worried about the anaconda.

After breakfast, Dad took the cover off the heating vent in the kitchen.

"What are you doing?" I asked.

"I'm checking to see if the ducts should be cleaned," he said. "I thought I heard a noise earlier. I hope it's not a mouse in there."

An alarm went off in my head. "Is a mouse a small mammal, Dad?" I asked.

"It sure is," Dad said. "And so are you," he added with a smile.

"Thanks for telling me, Dad," I called over my shoulder as I left the room. I wasn't enjoying our discussion anymore.

I went to my room and shut the door. After my routine security check for the anaconda, I flopped into bed. I was beginning to think that the anaconda might have eaten George.

Then I started to think about the other animals in our neighborhood. The Gomez family on the other side of us has a large black dog, and the O'Gradys next to them have an orange cat and two hamsters. Ryan and Brett have a dog and a bird. The Andersons across the street have a poodle named Sassy, about the same size as a cat. The only other animal at our end of the street is Whiskers, a skinny black cat that belongs to Mrs. Cooper. All those pets could be in danger if the anaconda had left the house!

I decided to get Jake's help in hunting down the anaconda. We spent the morning searching the whole house. We started in the basement and worked our way up to the bedrooms. We looked in, under, and behind everything in every single room. We had to do it together because we were afraid of finding something we didn't want to see. We didn't find an anaconda.

"It must have gone back when you tapped the picture twice," Jake said with a sigh of relief.

Just then, Amanda rushed in all flustered.

"Did you hear that the O'Gradys' cat, Rosie, has disappeared?" she panted.

Oh no! I thought to myself.

"Oh no!" Mom said. "Any news about George? Is he back?"

"Not a sign," Amanda said. "He's still missing."

"George and Rosie must have run away together," Jake said, flashing a feeble grin.

Amanda glared at him. "For your information,

smarty-pants, Rosie got out when the O'Gradys had a new mattress delivered this morning. But she hasn't come back."

"We should make some 'Missing Animal' posters," Jake suggested, obviously feeling guilty about his joke. "The O'Gradys and the Hamiltons might offer rewards for their missing cats."

"Great idea!" Amanda cried. "Jake and I can design the posters after lunch. We'll go and ask about a reward."

Amanda and Jake took off right after lunch, leaving me alone. I was so sick of my chicken pox! I couldn't even play with my friend Brett, who had the chicken pox, too. He was still in the staying-in-bed stage. Thanks to all those stupid spots, I didn't get to do *anything*!

Chapter Six

Mysterious Ripples in the Pool

With nothing better to do, I decided to read Jake's book on snakes. It said that the anaconda liked water as well as trees. I looked out the window into the backyard. I couldn't see anything like a snake on the branches. Then I focused my gaze on the swimming pool. It looked like one end of the plastic pool cover was turned back where the wind had lifted it. The gap was big enough for a snake to slide into the pool!

I rushed downstairs and out into the backyard, being careful where I stepped. I lay down at the edge of the pool and gently lifted the cover to peer in. I dropped it fast! It looked like something green and curly was swimming in the water! I dropped a brick on top of the cover and ran inside as fast as I could.

I was trying to calm down when Jake and Amanda returned with the posters they had made. Under a large **LOST** heading were photographs and descriptions of the two missing cats. At the bottom it said in large print:

REWARD OF $5 FOR EACH CAT RETURNED TO OWNER.

"That's a great poster," Mom said.

"Thanks," Amanda replied. "All the kids on the block are looking for the two cats. We're going to put posters on the telephone poles on Maple, Oak, Ash, and Elm streets."

"You should put one in the pet store," I suggested. "The Pet Place. They have a bulletin board at the front of the store."

"Great idea, Max! I'll go right now," Amanda said.

Jake turned to go with her, but I grabbed his arm. "I have to tell you something," I whispered to him. "In private. *Now!*"

Jake followed me into the den. "What's the matter with you?" he asked.

"I think it's in the pool," I whispered. "I saw something swimming under the cover."

"Are you sure?" Jake asked. "I'd better go and see if it's really an anaconda."

We went into the backyard and walked over to the pool. I showed Jake the brick I'd put on the cover to hold it down.

"Be careful when you lift up the cover," I said. "It might leap out at us."

Jake removed the brick. Then he lay down and raised the edge of the cover. He looked inside and suddenly yelped! He dropped the cover and yelled out, "Get a whole bunch of bricks! It's real long and green. I saw its tail, so its head must be out in the middle of the pool."

Dad was planning to build a barbecue pit when the weather got warm. He had a pile of bricks by the fence. We ran over and grabbed some of the bricks. As quickly as we could, we placed a row of bricks along the entire edge of the cover. We didn't leave any space for the anaconda to wriggle through.

"Great! Now it's trapped," Jake said, panting. "You *did* get one, after all. Now the problem is, how are we going to get rid of it?"

"We've got some time to think about it," I said. "It

must be sleepy and full if it's already eaten two cats."

A ripple of wind blew across the yard, and something brushed against the pool cover—something long and twisting.

"I'm really thirsty," Jake said, watching the cover move. "I think I'll go inside and get a glass of water." He headed toward the house fast.

I prayed the cover would be strong enough to keep a large snake inside.

Chapter Seven

Wanted: One Bright Idea

"We'd better tell Amanda about the anaconda, Jake," I said as we gulped down our water. "She was very helpful with Penny and Angel."

Jake nodded. "Yeah, I guess it's time."

We went to look for Amanda, but she wasn't in the house. We found Mom and Dad reading in the den.

"Where's Amanda?" Jake asked.

"She's out with Molly, following up a lead about one of the cats," Mom said. "Someone called the Hamiltons and said they had seen a gray cat on Ash Street. Amanda went with the kids to see if it was George."

Jake and I both shook our heads. Neither of us thought anyone would ever see George or Rosie again, but we couldn't tell anyone why.

When Amanda came home at about five o'clock, she looked very tired. She sank into the sofa with a sigh.

"Hi guys," she said. "Sad news. The gray cat wasn't George after all, even though it *did* look a lot like him. Mrs. Hamilton took us to The Pet Place on Fairfield to put the poster on the bulletin board. Guess what they had in a big cage?"

"A snake?" I suggested.

"How did you know?" Amanda asked.

"I've been thinking a lot about snakes lately," I said. I looked over at Jake and he nodded. So I told Amanda the whole story about the anaconda. Her eyes grew wide with fear.

"Anaconda?" she stuttered, sitting upright. "Were you crazy? Where is it now? Will it eat us, too?"

"Calm down, Amanda," Jake said. "It's trapped in the pool, under the plastic cover."

Amanda glared at us. "Really?"

We both nodded.

"Isn't an anaconda like a python?" she asked. "That's what was in the pet store."

I nodded. "They are alike. What did they feed the python in the pet store?"

"The owner said it eats mice and rats. Molly said she'd like a python, now that they haven't got a cat."

Jake laughed. "She could have both!"

"That's gross," I said with a shudder.

"What do you mean?" Amanda asked. Then she realized what Jake was talking about. "Oh no! You don't mean that the anaconda ate George? That's terrible! Wait a minute. And then it swallowed Rosie?"

"We think one was dinner and the other was breakfast," Jake said.

"That's truly disgusting!" Amanda said. "What do we tell Molly, Lauren, and Spenser?"

"We don't tell them anything," Jake said. "They'll freak out if they think we have an anaconda in our pool."

"Are you sure it's there?" Amanda asked.

"Absolutely! Max saw it, and so did I," Jake said. "It's very long and olive green, just like the book said."

"We built a brick wall around the pool on top of the cover," I told her. "I don't think the anaconda can get out now."

"Well? What are you going to do about it?" Amanda demanded. "You'd better get rid of it before it chomps up all the pets in the neighborhood!" She was really upset.

I groaned. "I know! I tried to make it disappear on

Friday, but it didn't work. Maybe you can help us again."

"We'd better do something fast," Amanda said. "I wonder what you could have done wrong? Maybe the animal has to be close to the amazing dictionary in order for the magic to work."

"You could be right," I said. "If the anaconda left Jake's room as soon as I called it up, then it was probably too far away when I tapped the picture again."

"Let's take the dictionary out to the pool and try again," Jake suggested. He ran upstairs for the amazing dictionary. Then we all trooped out to the pool.

We were relieved to see that the bricks on the pool cover were still in place. But something was wriggling around under the cover.

"Oh boy!" Amanda said nervously. "It looks restless. It must be trying to get out!"

She turned to me. "You tap the picture, Max. Maybe the one who summoned the animal has to make it disappear."

I took the dictionary from Jake and turned to the picture of the anaconda. Keeping one eye on the pool cover and the other on the picture, I tapped it twice.

The pool cover swung up and then settled back down again.

"You try now, Jake," Amanda suggested. "After all, the dictionary belongs to you."

Jake took the dictionary from me and tapped the anaconda drawing once, and then a second time. Another ripple ran across the pool under the cover.

"It's not working," Amanda said, frowning.

"That's obvious," Jake shot back. "Does anybody have any other bright ideas?" He was getting impatient.

"Maybe the snake has to be in your room in order for the spell to work," I suggested.

"That's just great," Jake said. "How are we going to get it from the pool to my room?"

We stared at the pool as the cover moved up and down. It was as if the anaconda knew we were watching, and it was teasing us.

Chapter Eight

How Do You Catch a Giant Anaconda? (*Very* Carefully!)

I was happy to return to school Monday morning. I didn't have to worry about snakes when I was there. My teacher, Mr. Sandhu, said it was good to have me back.

Brett's seat was empty, and Emma, who usually sits across from me, was absent, too.

"You really spread the spots around, Max," Mr. Sandhu said. "Jenny was the only one in your group who didn't get chicken pox."

Mr. Sandhu gave me the work I had missed and showed me what I had to do to catch up with the rest of the class. "You should start first with this project on snakes," he said.

Snakes! I looked at the pile of papers and felt sick all over again. And to think, I had gone to school to get away from them!

"Can I do my project on the anaconda?" I asked.

"Why don't you choose an American snake, instead?" Mr. Sandhu suggested. "A grass snake or some other reptile that you might actually see."

"I feel very close to the anaconda," I said. "It's almost as though I could see one."

Mr. Sandhu gave me a strange look, but he wrote down "Anaconda" next to my name in his book. "As you wish, Max," he said. "The project is due on Friday, but you can have more time if you need it, since you've been sick."

After lunch, Mr. Sandhu gave me time to work in the library. I found a really good book on boa constrictors, pythons, and anacondas. It had colorful photos of the snakes. They were coiled up in piles and curled around the branches of a tree. In one picture, a python was swallowing a small animal that looked like a guinea pig. In the next picture, I could see a bulge in the snake where the guinea pig had gone. I wondered how big a bulge George and

Rosie made when the anaconda swallowed them.

Jake and I walked home together after school. We usually walked with Ryan and Brett, but Ryan had caught chicken pox, either from his brother or from me.

"I was thinking about your anaconda in the pool," Jake said. "It might freeze at night and die. They live in hot rainforests."

"I sure hope so," I said. "We should check and see if it's still moving."

We went around to the backyard as soon as we got home. The pool cover rose and dipped, as if to say "Hi!" The anaconda was still there. And it was very much alive.

Amanda came out to join us, munching on an apple. "How will we catch a big snake?" she asked.

"Very carefully," Jake answered, smiling.

Amanda scowled at him. "It would be very heavy," she said. "Carrying it is going to be tricky."

"Catching it will be even trickier," Jake said. "Are you volunteering for the job?"

"It's Max's snake," Amanda said. "Let *him* catch it."

"I'm only eight," I whined. "I'm too young to catch an anaconda. And I'm still weak from the chicken pox."

"Oh, poor little baby," Amanda said mockingly as she dropped her apple core down my back. She ran back into the kitchen before I could throw the core at her.

"Don't worry, Max, I'll help you," Jake said. "But how are we going to get it?"

"Mr. Sandhu tells us to problem-solve when we don't know what to do," I told him.

"Well, we'd better solve this problem fast," Jake said.

After dinner, I read a few chapters of the snake book for my school project. Then Mom said I could watch some TV before I went to bed. Amanda and Jake were already in the den.

"Turn to Channel Eight," Amanda said.

"But it's time for the basketball game," Jake protested.

"You'll really like what's on eight," Amanda insisted. "Look in the *TV Guide*."

"The Wild Dangerous World," Jake read. "Catching Boas in South America."

Amanda clicked on Channel Eight. A team of naturalists was in the Amazon jungle. They were trying to capture a giant boa to take back and study. They tracked a very large anaconda at the edge of a river. It was squeezing a fish in its coils.

The naturalists cornered the huge snake, and while it was watching the people in front, one guy pinned its head from behind and some others held it down. Then they all shoved it into an enormous bag.

"That's how the pros do it, guys," Amanda smirked at us. "Do you think you'll be able to handle it?"

"We have to get it out of the pool first," Jake said. I shook my head. It definitely was *not* a task I looked forward to.

Mom came in just then and ordered me to bed. While I was brushing my teeth, I began brainstorming for a solution to the anaconda problem. Mr. Sandhu had told us to simply come up with as many ideas as we could whenever we were faced with a problem.

Suddenly, a great idea came to me! I was so excited, I almost swallowed my toothbrush.

"Jake!" I yelled. "Jake! Come up here! I've got it! I've got it!"

Jake stomped up the stairs. "What's the matter?" he grumbled. "The basketball game's about to end."

"We need bait!" I said.

"Bait?" Jake looked puzzled. "Like worms and stuff?"

"Not fishing bait," I said. "I mean bait to attract the anaconda. What did it eat before it went into the pool?"

"George and Rosie."

"Exactly. It likes cats. So we get another cat as our bait."

"I don't know. It might work," Jake said. "But what if it eats the bait, too? We're running out of cats in our neighborhood."

I hadn't thought of that. "Can you tell Amanda about my idea?" I asked him. "Maybe she'll know where we can find a cat."

Chapter Nine

Bait for the Boa

At breakfast on Tuesday, Mom said she had a meeting downtown and told us we'd have to eat lunch at school. Amanda grabbed the last two pieces of cold pizza from the fridge. Jake and I had to settle for ham sandwiches.

On the way to school, I reminded Jake that we had to get a cat or a small dog into our backyard to lure the anaconda out of the pool.

"Whiskers is the only cat left," he said. "Mrs. Cooper has been watching him very carefully since George and Rosie disappeared."

"Amanda will help us," Jake said. "Let's meet in the backyard after school."

I thought about cats and snakes most of the day. I couldn't wait to get home and settle the anaconda

problem in our pool. During our math class, my mind
was so far away that I didn't see Mr. Sandhu standing
over me until he tapped me on the shoulder.

"Hello Max! Are you here?"

I jumped and stuttered, "I was problem-solving, sir."

"Better solve your math problems before you take on
the problems of the world," Mr. Sandhu replied sternly.
"You have a lot to do."

Jake and I rushed home as soon as school was over. We found Amanda and went out to the pool to think of ways to get Whiskers into our yard. Amanda and I were arguing over our ideas when Jake whispered, "Quiet! Look who's here." We turned around, and there was Whiskers digging in our vegetable garden!

"Quick, Max. Get that old cage off the shelf in the garage," Amanda ordered. She walked toward Whiskers, holding out her hand.

"Here, kitty, kitty," she said softly.

I grabbed the cage and made a fast detour into the kitchen to snatch some ham from the fridge. Whiskers was watching Amanda suspiciously. I crept up behind the cat and set the open cage on the ground.

I threw a little piece of the ham near Whiskers. She sniffed the ham and then ate it. I tossed another piece closer to the cage, and the cat gobbled that as well. I threw the third piece into the cage. Whiskers walked in after it. Amanda shut the door and latched it!

We looked around to make sure no one had seen us. Then we carried the cage over to the pool. We knew the snake couldn't swallow the cage, so we thought Whiskers would be safe.

Amanda was very brave. She took three bricks off the cover and pulled it open. As Jake and I moved back, Amanda grabbed an old rake and held it up high over the opening.

"I'll get it when it comes out!" she said. "I'll pin it on the ground, and you two can shove it into the bag. Get ready!"

Jake and I watched the pool. The anaconda didn't slither out. It didn't even move. We waited another five minutes. Still, nothing happened.

"Maybe it's dead," Jake said.

Amanda put down the rake. "Let's have a look under the cover," she said.

Before we could decide who should do that, Molly came through the gate between our yards. "What are you doing with Whiskers?" she asked all of us. "Why is she in that cage?"

"We found her wandering around," Jake said quickly. "We put her in this cage to keep her safe."

"We're taking her back to Mrs. Cooper," Amanda piped in. "You can help us."

"Okay," Molly said.

I replaced the bricks on the pool cover. Then the four of us carried the cage across the street to Mrs. Cooper's house.

Chapter Ten

All's Well That Ends Well

Mrs. Cooper was very pleased to see Whiskers. She hugged her and gave her some milk.

"Thank you, children," she said. "I don't know what I'd have done if Whiskers had been catnapped."

"Catnapped?" we asked.

"That's right," Mrs. Cooper said. "Haven't you heard? There's a gang of catnappers in the area. They're picking up cats and then selling them to pet stores and labs. Mrs. O'Grady is really worried about Rosie. She's a very expensive cat, and she won third prize once in a show. She's just the sort of cat the catnappers want."

Molly was upset to hear about the gang of catnappers. She rushed home to tell her parents all about it.

Mrs. Cooper gave us a chocolate bar as a reward for

finding Whiskers. She said she'd keep
the cat inside until the catnappers
were caught.

We said good-bye to her and took
the cage back to our garage. Then
we went and sat on our front porch.

"Now what?" Amanda asked, breaking
the chocolate bar into three pieces.

"Even if the anaconda is dead," Jake said, "we still have
to get it out of the pool before summer. I'm not
swimming with a stinky snake in the water."

Amanda agreed. "Dad will want to know how it got
there if we leave it," she said.

"The garbage is picked up on Thursday," I said. "If we
pull the snake out tomorrow night, we can stuff it in a
garbage bag. Nobody will ever know."

"You'd better bring a knife," Amanda said gloomily. "It
won't be easy to fit the anaconda into a bag."

After many cool days, Wednesday was suddenly very hot.

We went to school in jeans and jackets, and by lunchtime we were roasting. It felt like summer.

When Dad came home from work that night, he clapped his hands and gave us a big smile. "Well guys! I think it's warm enough to start thinking about swimming," he said.

"Oh no, Dad," Jake said. "It's too early for the pool."

"What do you mean, too early?" Dad said, clearly surprised. "You asked me to take the cover off the pool when we had that thaw in February!"

"But now I'm freezing," Jake said, rubbing his hands together.

"I've never heard you say you didn't want to swim," Dad told him. "You kids can help me take the cover off after dinner. We should check on the pool, now that winter is over."

"I have to do homework with Molly," Amanda said quickly.

Jake was equally quick with his excuse. "Lauren and

Spenser are going to shoot baskets with me and Max," he said.

Dad looked at us sternly. "I want your help with the cover. It won't take long, and then you can do your homework, Amanda, and you boys can shoot baskets."

We were so worried, we could hardly eat dinner, and there wasn't much conversation. When everything had been cleared from the table, Dad said, "Come on, everybody, let's open that pool."

We followed Dad into the backyard, walking as slowly as we could. He stared at the bricks on the pool cover.

"Who put all those bricks there?" he asked.

Amanda came up with a quick reply. "Jake and Max. The wind was lifting the cover, and they wanted it to lie flat."

Dad looked at us, clearly surprised. "Good thinking, guys," he said. "Now put the bricks back where you found them."

We took as long as possible to carry the bricks across

the grass and stack them in a neat pile. Then we moved slowly away from the pool. Dad spotted us and shouted, "Come on, kids! You can't help me from way over there. Grab an edge of this cover."

Amanda and Jake lifted the far side, and Dad and I took the edge near the house.

"Now carefully pull it along," Dad said.

We rolled the cover toward the center of the pool. Suddenly, something long and green shot out of the water and flew through the air. Without another thought, I ran for my life. Amanda and Jake climbed over the gate and ran into the Hamiltons' yard.

That's when I heard Dad yell, "Get it off me!" I froze, realizing Dad could be in trouble. I turned around and saw Dad and the anaconda tangled up together on the ground. Dad was making strange noises. The boa was crushing him!

I grabbed the rake that was leaning against the house and rushed to save my dad. Amanda climbed back over the fence, carrying a baseball bat she'd picked up. Jake waved a thick branch over his head.

Dad yelled again, "Help! Get it off me!"

But he wasn't choking, after all. He was laughing! I dropped the rake and picked up what turned out to be a garden hose! It was long, olive green, and curly.

"The hose?" Jake and Amanda gasped.

Dad wiped tears of laughter from his eyes. "What did you think it was?" he asked. "I've never seen any one of you move so fast."

"We were surprised!" I panted. My heart was thumping
so loudly, I felt as though a herd of bulls was running
across my chest.

Amanda pulled the rest of the hose out of the pool.
"Kids are easily frightened," she said with a big grin.

"You went right over the fence, yourself," I said.

"Don't tell me you weren't scared."

"I was only protecting Jake," Amanda countered.

"When he climbed over the fence, I went to help him."

"Right," I said. I burst into laughter, and soon Amanda

and Jake were rolling in laughter, too. We were so relieved. We didn't have to explain away an anaconda, after all.

"Are you guys okay?" Dad asked, looking at us with a puzzled expression on his face. "Come on, settle down and let's open up this pool."

We pulled back the rest of the cover. Suddenly the pool looked really, really good.

We were all showered and ready for bed when Molly came over, carrying George the cat.

"Look who's home!" she announced.

"Awesome!" we shouted in one voice.

"Where did you find him?" Mom asked.

"A woman on Elm Street had him at her house," Molly said. "She thought he was a stray cat and was keeping him. She fed him very well."

We all fussed over George as he purred happily and enjoyed all the attention.

"Now, if Rosie would just show up, everyone would be happy," I said.

Just then, the phone rang. Mom picked it up. After a minute or so, she hung up and said with a big smile, "Rosie has turned up."

"Cool!" I shouted.

"Where was she?" Amanda asked.

"She went off in the mattress delivery truck, hidden in a box," Mom explained. "The mattress people didn't know where she'd come from, so they called every customer they'd delivered to during the last week."

"I'm sure glad we don't have any more problems to worry about," Jake said.

"Oh yes, you do, Jake," I said.

"What?" Jake asked.

"Go look in the mirror," I said, stifling my laughter.

Jake rushed off to the bathroom. After a silent pause, we heard a loud yell.

"Nooooo!"

"What's the matter with Jake?" Mom asked.

"He's got chicken pox," I said, smiling.

Anaconda Fact Sheet

- Anacondas are the largest snakes in the world.

- They can grow to be thirty-six feet long and forty-four inches wide. Mature anacondas can weigh up to 1,100 pounds.

- Anacondas live in South America and belong to the Boa family.

- They like to live near freshwater habitats, such as rivers and lakes.

- They swallow their food whole, starting with the head.

- Their jaws come unhinged so that they can open their mouths very wide before swallowing their prey.

- They eat small animals as well as deer and pigs.

- They can live up to eighteen years.

For more information on anacondas, check out some of the amazing snake websites on the Internet. Try going to a search engine and typing in the word *anaconda* to see what you can find!

Using a Dictionary

You become a better reader and writer when you learn new words. Words become yours when you understand what they mean and use them in your writing and discussions.

Use a dictionary to look up any words in this book that you don't understand. You might want to start your own personal list of new words in a journal, or in a file in your computer. First, write down the definition of the word. Then use the word in a short sentence. The next time you write a short story, or an essay, try to use new words that you have learned. You will be amazed at how quickly you can expand your vocabulary this way.